D0177592

OUR ANGRY PLANET

Tsunamis

NICOLA BARBER

Adapted from an original text by Anne Rooney

FRANKLIN WATTS
LONDON•SYDNEY

First published in 2009 by Franklin Watts

Copyright © 2009 Arcturus Publishing Limited

Franklin Watts
338 Euston Road
London NW1 3BH

Franklin Watts Australia
Level 17/207 Kent Street, Sydney, NSW 2000

Produced by Arcturus Publishing Limited,
26/27 Bickels Yard, 151–153 Bermondsey Street, London SE1 3HA

Our Angry Planet is based on the series *Nature's Fury*, published by Franklin Watts.

Editor: Alex Woolf
Designer: Mind's Eye Design and Mike Reynolds

Picture Credits
Corbis: 4, 7, 16 (Punit Paranjpe/Reuters), 18 (Kim Kyung-Hoon/Reuters), 22 (Lloyd Cluff), 23 (Sukree Sukplang/Reuters), 24 (Babu/Reuters), 26 (Wolfgang Kaehler), 27 (Bazuki Muhammad/Reuters).
Rex Features: 10 (Sipa Press), 14 (Sipa Press), 15 (Sipa Press), 17, 19, 20 (SS/Keystone USA), 21, 29 (Twentieth Century Fox/Everett).
Science Photo Library: 5 (Chris Butler), 6 (US Geological Survey), 8 (Gary Hincks), 9, 11 (David Hardy), 12 (Sally Bensusen), 13 (Carlos Munoz-Yague/LDG/Eurelios), 28 (John Foster).
Zul Mukhida: 25.
Shutterstock: cover (Fouquin).

Every attempt has been made to clear copyright. Should there be any inadvertent omission, please apply to the publisher for rectification.

A CIP catalogue record for this book is available from the British Library.

Dewey Decimal Classification Number: 551.47'024

ISBN 978 0 7496 9050 2

Printed in China

Franklin Watts is a division of Hachette Children's Books, an Hachette UK Company
www.hachette.co.uk

Contents

What is a **Tsunami?**

A tsunami is a huge wave that can flood the land. The word *tsunami* is Japanese for 'harbour wave'. Tsunamis can hit towns and villages with little warning. These huge waves often destroy everything in their path, killing both people and animals.

Tsunamis through time

One of the earliest descriptions of a tsunami is by an ancient Greek historian called Thucydides. He used these words to describe a giant wave in the Mediterranean Sea near Greece in 426 BCE: 'the sea ... returned in a huge wave and invaded a great part of the town, and retreated leaving some of it still underwater; so that what was once land is now sea ...'.

▼ **Flooded houses in Hawaii, USA, in 1957. The floods were caused by a tsunami.**

What causes tsunamis?

Tsunamis are caused by a disturbance in or under the sea. The disturbance makes a lot of water move suddenly. Most tsunamis happen because of **earthquakes**. Sometimes **landslides** or volcanic **eruptions** can cause tsunamis.

▲ A tsunami destroys everything in its path.

CASE STUDY

When the sky and sea fell

The people of Burragorang in New South Wales, Australia, tell this story: one hot night, the sky tumbled and crashed down on the people below. A gigantic, burning star tore apart the ground and showered the people with chunks of earth and rock. Later, other people told of the ocean falling on them from above. The whole land was flooded. Today, scientists think that these events were caused by a **meteorite** falling into the Tasman Sea. The meteorite probably set off a tsunami. This happened between 500 and 850 years ago.

The **Tsunami Zone**

Most tsunamis happen around the Pacific Ocean. This is because volcanic **eruptions** and **earthquakes** are very common around the edges of the Pacific. Both eruptions and earthquakes can set off tsunamis that spread across the whole ocean.

Inland tsunamis

Although most tsunamis are in the Pacific, they can happen anywhere. There have been many tsunamis in the Mediterranean Sea. These tsunamis are often caused by earthquakes and volcanic eruptions around Italy and Greece.

Rivers and lakes can also be affected by tsunamis. In 1811 a massive earthquake struck New Madrid in the USA. The earthquake caused huge waves on the Mississippi River. In 1980 a volcano called Mount Saint Helens erupted in Washington State in the USA. Some of the ash and rock from the eruption fell into nearby Spirit Lake and set off a tsunami.

Pacific Ocean

▲ **The red areas on this map show where earthquakes and volcanic eruptions happen around the edge of the Pacific Ocean.**

Long-distance tsunamis

Sometimes a tsunami strikes land a long way from the event that causes it. In 1946 an earthquake in the Aleutian Trench, off the coast of Alaska, set off a tsunami. Five hours later the tsunami reached the Hawaiian Islands. These islands are in the middle of the Pacific Ocean – 4,000 kilometres away.

EARTH'S JIGSAW

The outer surface of Earth is called the **crust**. It is divided into chunks called **tectonic plates**. These plates fit together like a giant jigsaw. There are seven large plates and several smaller ones. Beneath the crust, red-hot rock moves very slowly, dragging the plates with it. As the plates move they rub and push against each other. This rubbing and pushing can cause earthquakes and volcanic eruptions.

▼ A man watches as the tsunami hits Hilo's Pier 1 in Hawaii in 1946. The tsunami destroyed the pier and swept the man away.

Earthquakes and Tsunamis

The Earth's **tectonic plates** move very slowly – about the same speed as your fingernails grow. However, sometimes the force of two plates pushing against each other makes them slip with a jolt. This movement causes an **earthquake**.

Earthquake area

Around the edge of the Pacific, the plates carrying the ocean push against the surrounding land plates. The land plates, called continental plates, force the oceanic plates downwards. Sometimes a piece of plate snaps off or flicks up, causing an earthquake. This sudden movement sends massive waves through the ocean above. Over the last 2,000 years, at least eight out of every ten tsunamis in the Pacific have been caused by earthquakes.

▶ Along the coastline the continental (land) plate forces the oceanic plate downwards. Earthquakes often happen along the joins between two plates.

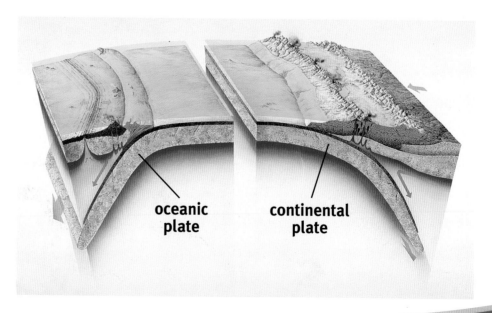

oceanic plate

continental plate

Land to sea

Earthquakes that happen on land but near a coast can also cause tsunamis. The earthquake sends waves through the solid ground, just like waves on water but slower. When the waves meet the sea, the movement transfers into the water. Some quite small earthquakes on land can set off huge and dangerous tsunamis.

◀ An earthquake destroyed much of Lisbon, Portugal, in 1755. Immediately after the earthquake, a tsunami hit the city.

CASE STUDY

Lisbon, 1755

On 1 November 1755, Lisbon in Portugal was hit by a very powerful earthquake. The earthquake lasted ten minutes and destroyed much of the city. People ran to the harbour to escape falling buildings. Then, minutes later, a tsunami struck. The huge wave swept many people away. More than 100,000 people died as a result of the earthquake and tsunami in Lisbon.

Volcanoes and Tsunamis

The movement of the Earth's **tectonic plates** also causes volcanic **eruptions**. As the continental plate pushes down the oceanic plate, the solid **crust** of the oceanic plate starts to melt. Far below the surface of the Earth, it turns into red-hot, liquid rock called **magma**.

▼ **This eruption happened on the island of Montserrat, in the Carribean, in 1997. Volcanic eruptions on Montserrat have often set off tsunamis.**

In some places the magma rises up towards the surface. It collects in vast spaces beneath the ground called **magma chambers**. When a magma chamber is full, the magma bursts through the Earth's crust. The magma explodes into the air, hurling out ash, rocks and gas. This is a volcanic eruption.

Water and fire

Many volcanoes lie along coasts or on islands. Sometimes during an eruption, water rushes into the magma chamber beneath the volcano. The mixture of water and red-hot rock can cause a violent explosion. The sudden movement of so much water can set off a tsunami.

Many volcanoes are completely underwater. When one of these volcanoes erupts, it pushes the water above it upwards. Sometimes the seabed collapses into an emptying magma chamber. Either event can cause a tsunami.

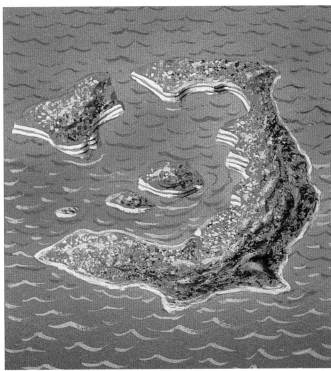

CASE STUDY

Krakatau, 1883

Krakatau is an island in Indonesia. In 1883 the island blew apart in a massive volcanic eruption. The eruption happened after a crack opened up in the volcano. Seawater poured in through the crack and onto the red-hot rock inside. The explosion left a huge hole where the island had been. As the sea rushed into this hole, it set off a tsunami. The tsunami swept over the coasts of surrounding islands. About 36,000 people died in the tsunami.

▲ The Greek island of Thera (Santorini) was a giant volcano (left) before it erupted in about 1410 BCE. Today the island looks like this (right).

Watery Build-Up

When an earthquake happens under the water, the seabed shakes. This movement transfers into the water above to make a series of waves.

The waves travel outwards in a circle from the **epicentre** (starting point) of the earthquake. The waves nearest the shore reach land quickly. This is called a local tsunami. Often there is no time to warn people about the approach of a local tsunami. Other waves may travel a long way before they hit land. Sometimes they cross the ocean to coasts many hundreds or even thousands of kilometres away. This is called a distant tsunami.

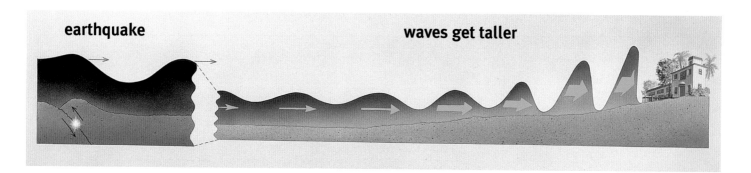

earthquake

waves get taller

▲ An earthquake on the seabed can set off a tsunami.

Starting small

Far out at sea, in deep water, a tsunami is a tiny wave. The wave may be only 60 centimetres high. Ships can sail over such waves without noticing them. But these low waves travel very fast – up to 750 kilometres per hour. As the tsunami gets nearer to land, the water gets shallower. The wave slows down and grows much taller. By the time it reaches the shore, it can be more than 30 metres high.

Spot a tsunami

	Normal wave	Tsunami
Speed	8–100 km per hour	800–1,000 km per hour
Wave period (time between two waves)	5–20 seconds	10 minutes to 2 hours
Wavelength (distance between two waves)	100–200 metres	100–500 km

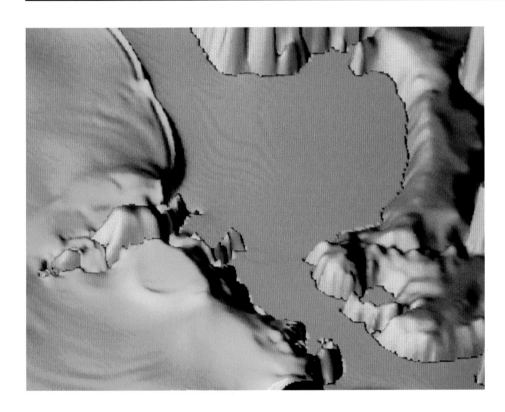

◀ **This computer picture shows the tsunami caused by the 1755 earthquake in Lisbon, Portugal.**

WHY DOES A TSUNAMI GROW SO TALL?

Out at sea the tsunami travels very fast. As it slows down, all of the fast-moving water in each wave piles up. As the water gets shallower, the waves get taller.

Minute by Minute

If people know that a tsunami is on its way, they can move to a safe distance before it arrives. But when a tsunami strikes without warning, it can kill many people.

▼ **ThIs satellite picture shows the sea drawing back from the coast of Sri Lanka in December 2004, just before a tsunami strike.**

Sometimes people along coasts can tell that a tsunami is on its way. This is because the sea draws back a very long way, much further than a normal low tide. This is the tsunami pulling the sea back into itself. There may be a hissing or sucking sound, then a rumble like thunder as the tsunami approaches.

Flooding

A tsunami is not usually a big breaking wave with a crest. Instead, a tsunami often looks like a giant wall of water. The level of the sea suddenly rises, and a flood sweeps in over the land. The shape of the coastline affects how the water behaves. If there are lots of bays and **promontories**, the water often flows in several different directions. Sometimes a harbour can trap a wave so that it bounces backwards and forwards off the harbour walls.

Wave after wave

Tsunamis are made up of several waves. The waves can follow each other at intervals of anything from five to 90 minutes. After the first wave of a tsunami, people sometimes return to the area. This is very dangerous because they may then be killed or swept away by the next wave.

▲ Water from a tsunami floods a village in Thailand in 2004.

 CRASHING WAVE

If a tsunami moves suddenly from deep to shallow water, it can form giant breaking waves. These waves are called **bores**. This can happen when a tsunami travels up a river.

Human Catastrophe

▼ Survivors of the 2004 tsunami look at their devastated home.

A tsunami can cause terrible devastation when it hits the shore. Many people live along coastlines where tsunamis can strike. Many tourists visit these places too.

Death and destruction

When a tsunami floods onto the land, many people may drown in the water. The water moves so fast that it can throw people against hard objects or against bits of wood and other **debris** carried along in the water. When the tsunami draws back out to sea again, people can be dragged out with it.

For those who survive, life after the tsunami is often a struggle. The power of the waves destroys buildings and crops. Survivors often have nowhere to live, no clean water to drink and nothing to eat. When the waters drop, the dead bodies of people and animals may lie unburied on the land. In these conditions there is a great danger of disease.

Cut off

The tsunami may sweep away roads, harbours and airport runways. This often makes it difficult to get help to the survivors. There may be no drinking water, food or medical help for several days, especially in remote areas.

CASE STUDY

Indian Ocean, 2004

On 26 December 2004 there was an **earthquake** in the Indian Ocean off the north-west coast of the Indonesian island of Sumatra. The earthquake set off the most devastating tsunami in human history. The tsunami hit coastlines all around the Indian Ocean with waves up to 30 metres high. The waves killed nearly 300,000 people. More than a million people lost their homes.

▲ A village near the coast of Sumatra, Indonesia, lies in ruins after the 2004 tsunami.

Helping Out

After a tsunami, people need help as quickly as possible. The emergency services try to rescue people who are in the water or who are trapped or injured. The next job is to provide food, shelter, water and medical help.

▼ A member of the US navy with a survivor of the 2004 tsunami. A US helicopter flew injured survivors to hospital.

Emergency services

The emergency services include the police, coastguards, ambulance and fire services. They are needed to rescue people from the water. They help people who are trapped under **debris** or inside collapsed buildings. They also have the grim task of removing dead bodies.

If the tsunami affects a wide area, local emergency services often cannot cope. Help from outside is needed. Emergency teams may come from overseas. The armed forces may also help. If places are cut off by water or by piles of debris, clearing roads into the disaster area is very important.

Keeping in touch

Mobile phones and computers are often vital for keeping in touch after a disaster. After the Indian Ocean tsunami of 2004, survivors and rescuers used text messages to find people who were trapped. They used blogs – diaries kept on a website – to keep the outside world updated.

▲ Survivors of the 2004 tsunami lived in these houses until their own homes were rebuilt.

CASE STUDY

Rescue and rebuilding

After the Indian Ocean tsunami of December 2004, emergency teams arrived quickly from overseas. They brought water purification units to clean water so that it was safe for drinking. They also brought tents, medicines, food and doctors and nurses. Countries around the world have also given money to rebuild the area. The estimated cost of clearing up and rebuilding is more than US$13 billion over several years.

Terrible Aftermath

The effects of a tsunami can last for years. For people who have lost family members, the effects last a lifetime.

Dead and missing

Many people lose a number of family members and friends during a tsunami. Many of the bodies of missing people are never found. When bodies are found, it is often impossible to identify them. Many children are left as orphans, without any parents.

After the tsunami of 2004, there were thousands of missing people. People put photos of their loved ones on internet sites to try to find them. There were also displays of missing people in local hospitals. These pictures helped to identify lost survivors and recovered bodies.

▶ **The scene in Phuket, Thailand, after the 2004 tsunami.**

Broken communities

A tsunami can also destroy buildings, farms, roads and forests along coasts. Afterwards it is often impossible for people to make a living. They have no houses and nowhere to work. In some places there are not enough people left alive to rebuild a community. Money and help from overseas is vital for helping people to rebuild their lives.

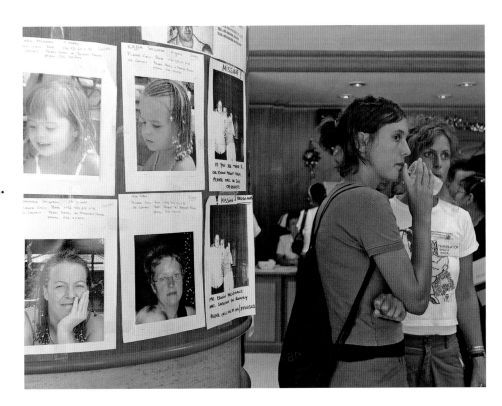

▲ A display of missing people in a hospital after the 2004 tsunami.

CASE STUDY

Papua New Guinea, 1998

On 17 July 1998 a tsunami swept across part of Papua New Guinea in the Pacific Ocean. The tsunami was ten metres high. It arrived without any warning after an **earthquake** nearby. Many children were playing on the beaches during the school holiday. They were swept away by the waves. A survivor described what happened: 'I felt the earthquake rocking the house. It was dark. Then we heard the sea break. I saw it, very huge; we tried to run but it was too late.'

Environmental Impact

After a tsunami, the first priority is to help people. But a tsunami can also cause great damage to the environment. This can be a particular problem in places where people live from fishing or farming.

▼ A tsunami in 1958 flattened trees more than 500 metres up the slopes of Lituya Bay, Alaska, USA.

Under the sea

The sea soon looks calm again after a tsunami. But beneath the surface there may be a lot of damage. A tsunami can smash apart **coral reefs** and move huge rocks. This can be very dangerous for fishermen who once knew the shape of the land under the sea.

During a tsunami, **debris** is often washed from the land into the sea. This debris may include the dead bodies of people and animals.

GROWING BACK

After a tsunami, plants soon start to grow again and animals soon return. In flattened forests, fast-growing trees start to appear within a year or two. They provide food for animals who start to move back in. Under the sea, repair is slower. It may take centuries for coral reefs to grow back after a major tsunami.

▼ The tsunami of 2004 flattened trees in Ban Nam Khen village in Thailand.

The debris floats into bays and harbours. As the dead bodies decay, they pollute the water. This pollution can poison fish and other sea life.

On land

On land, the huge waves of the tsunami can flatten forests and flood farmland. The salt in seawater may also ruin farmland. It can take years for the soil to recover so that farmers can grow crops.

In some places people have removed natural barriers such as coral reefs and **mangrove** forests. These barriers help to protect the coast from tsunamis. Without these barriers a tsunami can sweep much further inland.

Rebuilding

▼ A man mends the roof of a house in India. The tsunami of 2004 destroyed the house.

It can take a very long time to recover from a big tsunami. The survivors need a lot of help to rebuild their communities.

Back to normal

It's very important for survivors to return to some sort of normal life as quickly as possible. The first priority is to get food, water and medicines to survivors. After that, people try to build some kind of shelter so that survivors have somewhere to live. It is also important for children to go to school. Helpers sometimes set up schools in tents or other temporary shelters.

Local people usually need help to rebuild. People come from all over the world to do whatever they can. They help to rebuild schools and hospitals, roads and harbours.

They also help to restore vital supplies such as water, electricity and communications such as telephone lines.

Making a living

It is vital that the survivors of a tsunami can make a living. People who live by fishing must always live near the coast. A tourist area will always need buildings on the seafront. People can only fully recover when they can support themselves.

▲ These teachers have come from overseas to help the survivors of the 2004 tsunami. This temporary school in Sri Lanka is in a tent.

CASE STUDY

Philippines, 1976

On 17 August 1976 an **earthquake** and tsunami killed more than 7,000 people in the Philippines. The tsunami caused most of the deaths when it swept away the whole of Pagadian City. People have now rebuilt Pagadian. Most of the houses in the city are made of wood, often on stilts. They were quick to rebuild, but another tsunami could easily sweep them away again.

Keeping an
Eye on Things

▼ Many people who live near the coast of Papua New Guinea have a tree that they can climb if a tsunami hits. They know they have somewhere safe to go if necessary.

Some places have early warning systems that detect **earthquakes** and possible tsunamis. Sirens and public address systems are used to warn people. However, there are many false alarms. It is not possible to tell whether a tsunami will actually follow an earthquake.

Seabed sensors

Remote warning systems are more accurate. These systems use **sensors** on the seabed. The sensors measure changes in the weight of water overhead. They can detect tsunamis far out at sea. The information goes to a **buoy** on the surface of the sea. It is then transmitted to a **satellite**. From the satellite it goes to a tsunami warning centre. From there, people can send warnings to the places likely to be affected.

Watching from space

Satellites in space are used to monitor the movement of Earth's **tectonic plates**. They can also spot any change of shape in the world's volcanoes.

This information can warn of possible earthquakes and **eruptions** that may trigger a tsunami.

Up against the wall

In some places people have built strong sea walls to hold back tsunamis. However, some experts believe that a powerful tsunami could smash these walls, or simply sweep over the top.

◄ **This new system uses text messages to warn people about earthquakes and tsunamis.**

AN INTERNATIONAL SYSTEM

The first tsunami warning centres were set up around the Pacific Ocean. But there was no system in place to warn people of the tsunami in the Indian Ocean in 2004. Since then, governments have started work on an early warning system for the Indian Ocean. An international tsunami warning system is now based in Hawaii, in the Pacific Ocean. It sends warnings all over the world.

Where Next?

Tsunamis are most likely to happen as a result of **earthquakes** or volcanic **eruptions**. But freak events can sometimes set off tsunamis.

▲ It is possible that a meteorite set off tsunamis that wiped out the dinosaurs. This happened 65 million years ago.

Mega-tsunamis

A mega-tsunami is a giant tsunami. Mega-tsunamis are often caused by huge **landslides**. A landslide happens when a mass of rock and soil slides down a slope. If the landslide hits water, it can set off a massive wave.

The largest wave ever recorded happened in Alaska, USA, in 1958. A landslide in Lituya Bay sent a massive wave more than 500 metres up the sides of the bay (see page 22). True mega-tsunamis are very rare events. The last known mega-tsunami happened 4,000 years ago at Réunion Island in the Indian Ocean.

From outer space

In the past, mega-tsunamis have been caused by **meteorites**. A meteorite is an object from outer space that hits the surface of Earth. If a meteorite lands in the sea, it can set off a tsunami. Scientists predict there is a one-in-300 chance of a huge meteorite hitting the Earth on 16 March 2880. It could cause a tsunami 120 metres high.

FUTURE THREAT

The volcano Cumbre Vieja lies on the island of La Palma in the Canary Islands. If the volcano erupts, it could send a huge landslide into the Atlantic Ocean. The landslide would set off a mega-tsunami that would race across the ocean. This gigantic wave would sweep away everything within 20 kilometres of the coast in North America and the Caribbean.

▼ **This shows what could happen if a mega-tsunami hit New York City.**

KILLER TSUNAMIS

When	Where	Why	Casualties
c.1410 BCE	Thera (Santorini), Greece	Volcanic eruption	c. 100,000 dead
20 September 1498	Nankaido, Japan	Earthquake	31,200 dead
28 October 1707	Tokaido-Nankaido, Japan	Earthquake	30,000 dead
22 May 1782	South China Sea	Earthquake	40,000 dead
13 August 1868	Northern Chile	Earthquake	25,674 dead
27 August 1883	Krakatau, Indonesia	Volcanic eruption	36,500 dead
15 June 1896	Sanriku, Japan	Earthquake	26,360 dead
26 December 2004	Indonesia	Earthquake	c. 290,000 dead

FURTHER INFORMATION

Books

American Disasters: Tsunami: Monster Waves by Mary Dodson Wade and Janet Hamilton (Enslow, 2002)

Horrible Geography: Cracking Coasts by Anita Ganeri (Scholastic, 2006)

Tsunami: Hope, Heroes and Incredible Stories of Survival by Joe Funk (editor), (Triumph Books, 2005)

Tsunami Man: Learning About Killer Waves with Walter Dudley by Anthony D Fredericks (University of Hawaii Press, 2002)

Tsunami: The World's Most Terrifying Natural Disaster by Geoff Tibballs (Carlton Books, 2005)

X-Treme Disasters That Changed America: Tsunami!: The 1946 Hilo Wave Of Terror by Scott Ingram (Bearport Publishing, 2005)

Websites

www.nationalgeographic.com/ngkids/9610/kwave/

news.bbc.co.uk/1/hi/in_depth/world/2004/asia_quake_disaster/default.stm

www.bbc.co.uk/science/horizon/2000/mega_tsunami.shtml

DVDs

The Day After Tomorrow directed by Robert Emmerich (Fox Home Entertainment, 2004)

Krakatoa, East of Java directed by Bernard L. Kowalski (MGM, 1969)

National Geographic: Tsunami – Killer Wave (Warner Home Video, 2005)

GLOSSARY

bore
A tsunami that arrives as a crashing, breaking wave.

buoy
An object that floats on the surface of water and is attached to the bottom to stop it drifting.

coral reef
A hard, underwater structure built by tiny creatures called coral.

crust
The hard, outer layer of the Earth.

debris
Fragments of something that has been destroyed or broken down.

earthquake
A sudden, violent shaking of the land caused by the movement of tectonic plates.

epicentre
The point on the Earth's surface directly above the place where an earthquake occurs.

eruption
When red-hot rock, gas and ash pours out of a volcano.

landslide
When a large mass of rock and soil slips down a slope.

magma
Red-hot, liquid rock beneath the surface of the Earth.

magma chamber
The area beneath a volcano in which magma collects.

mangrove
A tropical forest that grows in flooded or very swampy land.

meteorite
A lump of rock, ice or metal from space that crashes into the surface of the Earth.

promontory
A piece of land that juts into the sea.

satellite
An object that orbits Earth in space. Some satellites are used to send information from one part of the world to another.

sensor
A device that detects a change in the environment around it, such as movement or heat, and transmits a signal as a result.

tectonic plates
Vast slabs of the Earth's crust that carry oceans and continents.

INDEX

Page numbers in **bold** refer to illustrations.

aid 16, 19, 21
Atlantic Ocean 29
Australia 5

bores 15, 31

Canary Islands 29
Chile 30
communications 18, 19, 20, 25, 26,
    27, **27**
coral reefs 22, 23, 31

disease 16
distant tsunamis 12

early warning systems 26, 27, **27**
earthquakes 5, 6, 7, 8–9, **9**, 12, **12**,
    17, 21, 25, 26, 27, 28, 30, 31
emergency relief 16, 18
environmental impact 22–23

farming 23
fishing 22, 25
flooding 4, **4**, **5**, 15, 16

Greece 4, 6, **11**, 30

homelessness and rehousing **19**,
    21, 24, 25

identification of living and dead
    20, **21**
India **24**
Indian Ocean 17, 19, 27, 28
Indonesia 11, 17, **17**, 30

inland tsunamis 6
Italy 6

Japan 30

landslides 5, 28, 31
local tsunamis 12

magma chamber 10, 31
medical treatment 16, 19
Mediterranean Sea 4, 6
mega-tsunamis 28, 29
    Réunion Island 28
meteorites 5, 28, 31

Pacific Ocean 6, **6**, 7, 8, 27
Papua New Guinea 21
Philippines 25
pollution 22, 23
Portugal 9, **9**
predicting tsunamis 26–27

rebuilding 19, 21, 24–25

satellites 26, 31
sea walls 27
Sri Lanka **14**, **25**

tectonic plates 7, 8, **8**, 10, 26, 31
Thailand **15**, **20**, **23**
tourism 16, 25
tsunamis
    Hawaii (1946) 7, **7**
    Hawaii (1957) **4**
    Indian Ocean (2004) **14**, **15**, **16**,

17, **17**, 18, **18**, 19, **19**, 20, **20**,
    21, **23**, **24**, **25**, 27, 30
Krakatau (1883) 11, 30
Lisbon (1755) 9, **9**, **13**
Lituya Bay, Alaska, USA (1958)
    22, 28
Mediterranean (426 BCE) 4
New Madrid, Missouri, USA
    (1811) 6
Papua New Guinea (1998) 21, **26**
Philippines (1976) 25
Spirit Lake, WA, USA (1980) 6
Thera (Santorini), Greece
    (c. 1410 BCE) **11**, 30
Tasman Sea (c. 1350–c. 1500) 5

USA **4**, 6, **7**, **22**, 28, **29**

volcanoes 5, 6, 7, 10–11, 26, 27,
    28, 29, 30, 31

waves 4, 9, 12, 13, 15, 17